Self Discipline & Time Management

Discover Powerful Strategies to Develop Everlasting Habits to Increase Productivity, Master Mental Toughness, Amplify Focus, and Achieve Your Goals!

Steve Martin

Copyright © 2022 by Steve Martin

All rights reserved.

No portion of this book may be reproduced in any form without written permission from the publisher or author, except as permitted by U.S. copyright law.

Contents

Image	1
Introduction	3
Self Discipline	
1. An Introduction To Self-Discipline	9
The Benefits of Self-Discipline	
Why Do You Want To Develop Self-Discipline?	
Living Your Life with Intent	
2. Habits	22
Self-Discipline Habits	
3. Free Goodwill	29
4. Mental Toughness	32
Visualization	

   Self-Talk

   Focus

   Concentration

   Mental Toughness and the US Military

5. Fear: The Destroyer of Your Persona, Self-Confidence, Self-Discipline, and Happiness   42

   Effects of Fear on the Body

   Effects of Fear on the Mind

   Fear is Our Teacher

   A Helpful Exercise

6. Daily Self-Discipline Tips   51

   Technique 1: Spartan Self-Discipline

   Technique 2: Navy SEAL Self-Discipline

   Everyday Tips

Final Words   67

Introduction   71

   Time Management

7. Time Management: What Does It Mean?   76

8. Managing Time and Goals   82

   Goals: Their Importance and How To Set Them

   Priorities: Define and Organize Them

   A Schedule: Create and Implement It

9. Stop Procrastinating by Concentrating   95
    Procrastination: Why It Happens
    What Are You Avoiding?
    Learn Why Concentration Is Important

10. The Influence of Your Smartphone   104
    How to Stop Wasting Time on Smartphones?
    How Can You Use Your Smartphone to Help You with Time Management?

11. Effective Time Management Principles, Techniques, and Tips   112
    The Pareto Principle
    The Pomodoro Technique
    Time Management and Productivity
    Learn How to Delegate
    Effective Time Management Tips

Final Words   126

Image   129

Refereces   130

"Without Discipline, nothing happens. I've found that discipline is the ability to give ourself a command and then follow it."

-Bob Proctor

Introduction

Self Discipline

Some people seem to have it all. They have great jobs, flawless bodies, and beautiful marriages. They even have the energy to go to the gym in the morning! Their self-belief is unshakable. When they want to accomplish something, they just do it. They seem to most of us to be godlike.

Okay, so I exaggerated a little. Nobody has a perfect life.

Some of us get quite close. What separates these fortunate individuals from the majority? What about them attracts success after success and opportunity after opportunity? You've probably observed that these outstanding individuals have a remarkable capacity to stay optimistic and stoic, even when everything around them falls apart.

Further, have you ever wondered how people who work and live in harsh environments keep going without giving up?

Some of them seem to enjoy the task! You've surely heard of Special Ops teams that spend weeks on near-impossible missions or adventurers who spend months trekking through freezing climes.

Other extraordinary people have lifestyles that need a different kind of extreme focus and concentration. A typical day in the life of a Zen Buddhist monk, for example, consists entirely of prayer and meditation. They reject the temptations of the earthly world and devote themselves entirely to spiritual growth. They are the religious counterparts of Olympic gymnasts and Fortune 500 CEOs. How can they maintain such a high level of motivation? What motivates them?

We may answer these issues with a single word: self-discipline.

It's not really about luck, you see. Sure, some individuals are born with genes that make them more attractive or happier than the typical person. But it's their laser-sharp concentration, tenacity, and the capacity to keep going when everyone else would give up that elevates a regular Joe or Jane to superhero status. You will discover their secrets in this book.

If you've ever wondered why you never seem to live up to your full potential, this is the book for you. If you're sitting on a pile of unfulfilled goals and ambitions, get ready to change your life! You're going to discover the secret that defines every successful athlete, CEO, and performer. You'll learn how some of the world's strongest people, including Navy SEALs and Spartans, consistently confronted danger and came out on top.

Why is this issue so important to me? I didn't realize the value of self-discipline until I was in my early thirties. I'd worked for several well-known firms, succeeding in most of my responsibilities in their human resources departments. But there was always something lacking. I felt as though I were losing control of my career. After all, no matter how big my position was, my work function and knowledge level were always chosen by someone else.

My normal pattern would be: I'd apply for an exciting new job, spend the first year getting to know the business culture, but then, around the 18-month mark, I'd get a growing sensation of claustrophobia. I'd become itchy. I'd fantasize about leaving my corporate job and becoming a freelancer. What would it be like to be my own boss? But every time I attempted to visualize truly starting my own company and accepting full responsibility for my life, I ran into a brick block. I couldn't seem to make a fresh start, no matter how much I wanted to. How would I keep myself motivated to look for new clients? Who would hold me accountable for my schedule? It all felt so overwhelming. As you can expect, I was nervous. I was at a fork in the road.

What eventually tipped the scales in my favor? One discussion helped. I was sitting at the coffee shop with a considerably older coworker one morning. He'd been in his position for over ten years and he despised it. We were chatting about the holidays we were going to take that year and I admitted that for a long time I'd wanted to start my company and travel the globe, going from country to country.

He burst out laughing. "Yeah, yeah," he said. "That's something no one ever does." A rush of disgust swept over me as he went back to his desk. So this is how losing feels, I reasoned. He is correct. That's something I couldn't do. It's all a dream. I don't think I've got it in me—or do I?

I had a decision to make. I could stay where I was, talking about the same difficulties and unmet dreams year after year, or I could make a drastic shift. I had a few self-help books on hand, some of which were unopened presents.

I immersed myself in the worlds of positive psychology and self-development and discovered how to accomplish anything I want. The answer to everything? Once again, it is self-discipline.

As it turned out, I had been asking the incorrect questions all along! I had maintained the conviction that in order to be successful, I needed to be entirely confident in myself and always driven by something. I also believed that if I became "successful," my life would miraculously fall into place and I would be happy. I had a lot to learn.

After many hours of studying, thinking, and testing, today I not only manage my own HR consulting firm, but I've also documented all of my favorite discoveries and top self-discipline ideas in this book. I don't want anybody else to be stopped by a lack of self-confidence or low self-discipline anymore. I am here to help!

You can improve your self-discipline and change your life if you truly want to. I currently live a life that is better than anything I could have envisioned a decade ago and I consider myself to be very self-disciplined.

I'm not flawless. I'll reveal a few of my own flaws as we go through this book—but the younger me would be shocked at how far I've come.

This book is divided into two sections. The first section will teach you all you need to know to change your thinking from self-doubt and ambivalence to complete self-discipline. You'll discover what psychology, philosophy, and even the military have to say about motivation and what pushes us to change.

The second section goes even further, focusing on the practical tactics you can start utilizing right now to supercharge every aspect of your life. You'll learn how routines, goal-setting, and a little-known technique called the Spartan self-discipline may help you push yourself harder than ever before.

Chapter 1

An Introduction To Self-Discipline

> The difference between great people and everyone else is that great people create their lives actively, while everyone else is created by their lives, passively waiting to see where life takes them next. The difference between the two is the difference between living fully and just existing.
>
> *-Michael E. Gerber*

John gets up at 5 a.m. every morning to work out. He works extremely hard at the office, ignoring distractions from his surroundings and devoting all of his attention to high-value projects. He takes a class in the evening; he will get his MBA in a few weeks.

How can people like John achieve so much consistently? And how can you achieve so much in your personal life and career? You may discover that a part of your solution is self-discipline.

There are several definitions of self-discipline. Before I outline the importance and advantages of self-discipline, I'd like you to get a piece of paper and a pen and write your own definition of self-discipline.

Compare that to my definition now that you've done it. For me, self-discipline signifies self-control, the capacity to stand out from the crowd due to distinctive habits and talents, and the elimination of everything that could end up producing bad outcomes for you.

It's no secret that the words "self" and "discipline" have an unpleasant connotation at first. In a nutshell, the two words suggest that we must "punish" or "discipline" ourselves in order to succeed. However, self-discipline is not about punishment.

Self-discipline is the capacity to control one's emotions and overcome one's flaws. It is also the capacity to pursue what one believes to be good despite temptations to abandon it. The act of self-discipline shows that one has passion and purpose (Duckworth, 2009). It demonstrates to other people that this person is prepared to do what is proper for them in terms of the outcome. It is never about what others infer; it is always about what you believe is proper or what you believe is your obligation.

The Benefits of Self-Discipline

I'm not going to lie to you. Life is difficult and it often throws you a curveball on your journey to success. This is unavoidable, but you can always do something about it and become powerful enough to tackle these problems as a professional and accomplish more than you believe you can.

With self-discipline, you can overcome these obstacles. This ability may bestow peace upon you and provide you with the tools you need to deal with any situation. It also provides you the opportunity to keep going and do whatever is in your power to achieve your goal, even if you feel like giving up.

Aside from the opportunity to rise and progress toward your goals, self-discipline is beneficial in a variety of other ways. It has a lot of advantages. Before I begin talking about them, I must tell you something else. You must understand that self-discipline is not just desirable when you are attempting to add something positive or successful to your life. This ability is also required to overcome any bad habit or addiction, such as smoking or drinking, and it is beneficial for overcoming many physical and mental health disorders (Ford, 2007).

While reading the book "The Chimp Paradox" by Dr. Steve Peters, I discovered that self-discipline offers people a basis for their character and inner strength. He made a fantastic remark that I still think about to this day. To be more precise, he emphasized in his book that you are already the person you want to be. The only thing that prevents you from realizing it is your emotional thinking. In fact, Dr. Peters claims that our emotional thoughts prevent us from behaving in the way we would prefer (Peters, 2020).

If you think about it for 60 seconds, you will understand that you are a compassionate and kind person, but that you easily lose your temper. Unfortunately, this situation will tell others that you are an angry person rather than one who is kind and caring. This does not imply that you must alter who you are to please others. All you have to do is adjust your behavior. People will see the real you this way and they will understand that you are not an angry person at all. You just have a bit of a temper. Dr. Peters used this example to help me understand the power of self-discipline. The skill enables people to better control their emotions and teaches them how to regulate their emotions as well.

Temptations, temptations, temptations. What's the matter with them? They are, in most cases, the reason why people lack self-discipline. Temptations, in fact, are the ones that throw people off course and keep them from attaining their goals (Gul & Pesendorfer, 2001). We don't understand that these temptations are just temporary, but the consequences of succumbing to them can be permanent. Self-discipline helps a lot here since it motivates people to tackle obstacles and continue on their journey. I've had a lot of problems with temptations at work. That's why I was so eager to discover a "cure." Specifically, I kept distracting myself with social media. I was constantly checking my phone, not understanding that it did not help but distract me. This gave me less time to do my work. Checking my phone was only one of the many distractions that I was facing. However, after discovering self-discipline, I understood the power of these distractions and started avoiding them. But I'll talk about myself later.

Jesse Wens once said that everyone in the world has a dream. However, in order for these dreams to come true, people must devote themselves, define themselves, and put maximum effort and self-discipline in them. This way, success is guaranteed. The third advantage of having self-discipline is a higher possibility of success. Don't get me wrong; every goal is challenging and requires sacrifice and growth. Growth does not happen overnight, yet it considerably improves your abilities, attitudes, and knowledge. Every obstacle that stands in the way of your goals may be overcome with self-discipline.

Who doesn't desire a positive relationship with their friends, family, or partner? Take out your pen and notebook once again. Now, write down what you look for in a relationship. To be more specific, what are the things that you value when it comes to your relationships with the people around you? I believe I know what you're going to write. Among others, you will most likely mention reliability, integrity, love, loyalty, and honesty. I know this since every person needs more or less the same thing when it comes to relationships. How can self-discipline assist in this situation? Self-discipline may assist you in developing better relationships by consistently displaying these character traits.

Self-disciplined people are self-assured, they can handle criticism, they always do their best, and most importantly, they never fail. In rare circumstances, if they do, they learn from their mistakes and see failure differently. It becomes an opportunity to improve themselves and become better.

Furthermore, we have been subjected to expectations and difficulties from the outside world from the day we were born. Some of our difficulties are self-inflicted, while others are imposed by other people or situations. In order to craft the life you really want to live, you must practice self-discipline.

Another important question is raised here. Do you understand why? Do you understand why you desire to develop self-discipline so much? Have you ever wondered what motivates you? Because, in order to develop self-discipline, you must first understand why you need it.

Why Do You Want To Develop Self-Discipline?

I felt like Captain America shortly after strengthening my self-discipline. This may sound like a joke, but it is real. I felt powerful enough to overcome any obstacle and pursue what I needed to live a great life and be successful. It wasn't easy in the beginning. I thought it was difficult because I hadn't learned and developed the right skills. But, as time passed, I understood the deeper issue. The issue was that I wasn't clear on why I wanted self-discipline. Yes, we all want to be better and we all want to get the skills to do that, but there is always something more than simply saying, "because I want to be better."

I sat down one day and began thinking about why I wanted this so much. My first thought was, "Because I want to be more successful in my work." Then I thought that I would love to improve my health, that I would love to stop procrastinating, that I would love to stop being distracted, that I would love to write more books, and more. Yes, I had a lot of problems that I had no clue how to fix.

You see, you need to figure out what your long-term goals are. Long-term goals are, in fact, the second takeaway of this book, apart from self-discipline. They are the motivators for you to stop being self-destructive and become disciplined.

This powerful "why" will compel you to stay on the road to success and remind you of it when confronted with a temptation. Let's imagine you wish to lose weight and get healthy. Your goals will not work if you are constantly tempted by unhealthy food. For instance, suppose someone offers you a slice of cake and you accept it. You say to yourself, I will eat this piece of cake because one piece of cake won't harm me. Why did you agree to take that piece of cake when you clearly said that you are on a diet? Why did this happen?

It happened because your goal isn't strong enough and it is not quite specific. In order to work toward your goals, you must first make them strong, specific, and easy to visualize. To be more precise, you must develop a powerful emotional response. Let's be a little more specific. Let's say you want to lose 20 pounds by the end of the year so you can wear your favorite dress or suit to a New Year's party. Consider how you would feel after wearing that dress or suit. How beautiful you will look and how healthy you will feel. Also, remember that you are the one in charge. You will be the one who determines what you eat and how much exercise you get each day.

Now, let's go back to that slice of cake. Is it worth it to give up this wonderful vision of yourself for a piece of cake filled with sugar? Instead, eat an apple and start feeling better by remembering that you are still in control.

However, there is one element lacking from the method I just taught you. Stop for a moment and consider your "why".

Consider everything you experience at that exact moment, not just what you smell or hear. You must concentrate on it for at least 60 seconds in order to remove your attention from the temptation (Gul & Pesendorfer, 2001). Your body will return to normal after a minute of slowing down. It will not surrender to the temptation. Remember, if you make an impulsive decision when faced with a need, your choice is unlikely to be aligned with your long-term goals.

Living Your Life with Intent

I've been obsessed with intentional living from the moment I discovered it. That is because it has really improved my life. In fact, I'd love to share my story with you and assist you to better understand the concept.

You know how life is for busy people, it's always "go, go, go." I used to be like that. My existence was nothing but always being on the go. We know this condition as living "life on autopilot." I was constantly feeling like I was falling behind, yet something deep within me was telling me that I was too busy to fully be living to begin with. Looking back, this was a clear indication that I needed to take a closer look—but I didn't. Instead, I found it easier to keep living on autopilot. I made life decisions (big and small) based on what everyone else was doing and I let the momentum of those choices drag me through life.

Intentional life begins with a "why" as well. You must once again ask yourself why you want to do things, but this time you must be satisfied with the replies. Here are some questions that may help you discover your "why":

1. Why do you spend time with your friend? Why are they your friends?

2. Why did you buy something (insert what)?

3. Why did you decide to become (insert a profession)?

4. Why are you with your partner?

5. Why do you work long hours?

6. Why do you wake up late?

After you've answered these questions, consider how these responses make you feel. Are they upsetting or perplexing you? Did you find it difficult to answer some of them? Intentional living entails examining your life choices. However, it is not about obtaining all that you want at that same moment. It indicates that you have a purpose or a goal.

To explain it better, here are two examples:

1. "I am taking a creative painting class because I want to be able to reproduce one of Vincent van Gogh's paintings before I turn 40."

2. "I am taking a creative painting class because I feel inspired when I explore my creativity and I am

considering painting a picture one day."

Both examples suggest intentional living. The first person has a plan, while the second person has no idea what they really want. Regardless of their different situations, one thing is clear. They live their lives intentionally. So, everything starts with your core values and vision.

Each person's core values are unique, and they are the key to selecting a proper goal. Keep in mind that every single person has different core values. For example, mine include care for my readers, care for myself, enormous amounts of self-discipline, time management, and freedom from the daily grind.

These values shape my life vision and explain my choices. So, the first step toward intentional living is defining your core values and your vision. Begin by recalling moments when you were joyful. Consider moments that made you the happiest or proudest person alive. Then start digging.

Chapter 2
Habits

Charles Duhigg is a reporter and the author of the award-winning book The Power of Habit. In it, he discusses scientific discoveries that illustrate how habits exist and how they may be changed (Duhigg, 2020). He aids us in understanding human nature and how we all have the potential to evolve.

Habits are the simple decisions we make and perform on a daily basis. They are responsible for the majority of our everyday activities. Our lives are a sum of our habits, but our habits aren't permanent. We all have some negative patterns that we follow and once we identify and break them, we make way for positive lifestyle changes. There are several strategies to change behavior, and they differ for each person. Habits are the foundation that leads to increased productivity and improved performance (Duhigg, 2020).

Break Bad Habits, Adopt Good Habits

MIT researchers illustrate how every behavior follows a neurological loop (The Massachusetts Institute of Technology, 2021). This contains three parts: a cue, a routine, and a reward. To understand your habits, you must first identify the habit loop of each of your behaviors. A feedback loop affects both positive and negative behaviors. To break negative habits or develop good habits, you must pay attention to what the loop is by employing the cue, action, and reward method.

- **Cue:** This is a trigger point that instructs your brain to go into autopilot mode and follow a set of instructions. Because we are continuously bombarded with information, identifying a cue may be challenging. Moreover, most habitual cues fall into one of the following categories: location, timing, emotional state, other people, and previous action. Assume that you eat a cookie every day, which contributes to your afternoon slump as well as weight gain. Note when you eat the cookie, what time you eat it, how you feel when you eat it, who else is around, and what you were doing right before you ate the cookie. This will assist you in isolating the cue that leads to the yearning. Are you seeking a diversion or is hunger driving your decision? Your response will determine the method to change the behavior. The cue is also a good place to start when developing a new habit. To start a routine, you must either create a new cue or identify one that already exists. For example, if you want to include exercise into your life, your cue may be wearing your jogging shoes every day after work at 6:30 p.m. This will set off the routine.

- **Routine:** This is another action that might be emotional, physical, or mental in nature. Disrupting the routine is an effective strategy to break a habit. You might keep the cue and reward while changing the routine. For example, if you are a smoker, smoking is a routine that may be triggered by stress (cue). Breaking the behavior might be as simple as doing something else when you are stressed (such as talking to someone or chewing gum).

- **Reward:** This, according to your brain, is what makes the routine worthwhile. When attempting to break a habit, experiment with several types of rewards. Take as much time as you need to find one that works for you. Rewards are psychological and the endorphin surge that accompanies them might make the current reward more appealing, even if it has negative consequences. Consider yourself a scientist gathering data points to test various hypotheses. Every time you attempt a new reward, write down your opinions about the experience. Are you satisfied? Does your finding make you nervous? Consider the values that are essential to you while looking for a reward. This way, you find the reward that works for you.

Once you've identified your loop, you can start shifting your behavior. You may either create a better routine and prepare for the cue or you can find a good reward. It's up to you. You need a strategy in any case.

So now that we understand how habits function, let's talk about how to break harmful behaviors and establish positive ones. It's worth emphasizing that if we attempt to change all of our negative behaviors all at once, we're going to fail and we'll end up feeling even worse than we did before. It's far better to focus on one habit at a time, work on it for a while, and then move on to another (Duhigg, 2020).

1. **Identify the reward:** The key to breaking a bad habit is to first identify what kind of reward we want when we respond to a trigger. Using our earlier example of afternoon snacking as an example, are you really hungry or do you need a diversion and a break from your desk?

2. **Find an alternative behavior:** Once we've identified what reward motivates us to act on a trigger, we'll be able to better understand how to change our behavior. If the reward you're looking for is reducing hunger and you want to cut down on the number of cookies you eat, consider keeping some healthy snacks at hand. A handful of unsalted mixed nuts, carrot sticks and hummus, a boiled egg, or natural Greek yogurt with berries are some examples of better snacks. When it gets close to 3 p.m. and you're hungry, head to the kitchen as usual, but instead of a cookie, have a healthy snack. If the reward you're looking for is a

diversion from your job, think about other methods to enjoy a break. You may have a brief conversation with a coworker, go outside and stroll around the block once, or make a cup of herbal tea.

3. **Practice:** The next step once you've identified the reward you're searching for is to practice and put a different behavior in place. Repeating the new habit loop over and over will eventually lead to this behavior requiring less willpower and becoming automatic.

Self-Discipline Habits

The major question is still unanswered as of yet. How can we enjoy self-discipline as a way of life, both personally and professionally, and what habits should we adopt?

We can start with the habit of commitment. Disciplined people keep their promises. When they make a decision, it's set in stone and they don't even need an accountability partner to keep them on track.

Then there's the habit of temptation avoidance. Isn't it difficult to resist temptation? So, guess what? It's difficult for everyone, even the most disciplined person. They are not always better at resisting temptation; they are just better at avoiding it altogether!

Last but least, there's the habit that makes you create new habits from time to time. Many people consider a disciplined life to be full of deprivation. But that's not a good way to look at it. Simply notice that you are forming a new habit, which takes time and energy to establish.

Chapter 3

Free Goodwill

People who help others (with zero expectations) experience higher levels of fulfillment, live longer and make more money. I'd like to give you the opportunity to convey this value during your reading or listening experience. In order to do so, I have a simple question for you...

Would you help someone you have never met if it did not cost you money, but you did not get credit for it?

If so, I have a 'request' to make on behalf of someone you do not know. And probably never will. They are just like you, or like you were a few years ago: less experienced, full of desire to help the world, looking for information but unsure where to look....this is where you come in.

The only way for me to accomplish my mission of helping other people is, first, by reaching them. And indeed, most people judge a book by its cover (and reviews). If you have found this book valuable so far, would you please take a brief moment right now and leave an honest review of the book and its contents? It will not cost you a dollar and less than 60 seconds.

Your review will help....

....one more person to find a way to improve their life.
....one more individual supports his or her family.
....one more friend experiencing a change they would never have experienced otherwise.
....one more life change for the better.

To make that happen...all you have to do is....and this takes less than 60 seconds....leave a review.

P.S. - If you feel good about helping faceless people, you are my kind of person. I'm really excited to help you improve in the coming chapters (you'll love the tactics I am about to share).

P.P.S. - Life hack: if you introduce something valuable to someone, they associate that value with you. If you'd like goodwill directly from another person - send them this book.

Thank you from the bottom of my heart. And now back to our regular program.

- Your biggest fan, *Steve*.

Chapter 4

Mental Toughness

Mental toughness is related to the study of performance psychology, and it was originally used to help elite athletes perform better. It emerged as a field of study in the mid-1980s and research continues to this day by developing mental toughness techniques and techniques to educate athletes, businesspeople, and all other types of performers to come up with breakthrough results.

The term "mental toughness" refers to the ability to persevere in the face of adversity while remaining positive and competitive. It also entails training and preparing yourself to be mentally prepared for whatever challenge comes your way (Jones, Hanton, & Connaughton, 2007).

Staying mentally strong will not only provide the strength we need to deal with our mistakes or poor performance, but it will also give us the resilience to keep going in the face of setbacks. When events don't go our way (or the way we want them to), we can't lose concentration or determination. We must continue to persevere through the adversity with which we are faced, according to the very definition of mental toughness.

Making routines, using visualization techniques, and practicing self-talk are all strategies to increase mental toughness.

Visualization

Visualization, according to top-performing athletes, is critical in maintaining and enhancing mental toughness before and during competitions (Jones, Hanton, &

Connaughton, 2007). Mark Plaatjes, a marathon runner and gold medalist, accomplished everything with the help of visualization and mental toughness. It is clear from his triumph in the 1993 World Championships Marathon that he has incredible mental toughness. Plaatjes was able to take the win with just three minutes to spare by studying images of the course and using visualization techniques to imagine himself running the course several times before the race.

The power of visualization, especially in athletic training, is mind-boggling, and makes it clear how useful it can be when used correctly. Using visualization correctly is clearly subjective, as each person benefits from different techniques. What worked for Mark Plaatjes may not work for you (Jones, Hanton, & Connaughton, 2007).

Regardless of individual differences, it is always necessary to visualize positive outcomes while being realistic and expecting the unexpected (good or bad). Visualizations should be detailed and outline exactly what you intend to achieve without opportunities for errors and changes in plans.

Finally, remain confident and calm while hoping for the best, even if the chances are stacked against you.

Remaining confident may seem simple, especially before a race or competition, but when the stakes are high, it is sometimes more difficult than it appears. In reality, it's quite easy to get discouraged as an athlete, especially if your performance hasn't met your expectations.

Self-Talk

Self-talk strategies have been demonstrated to increase confidence and improve mental toughness in a variety of situations, from the workplace to the court, track, or field.

Individuals may improve their performance by reframing critiques and using motivating self-talk. Developing personal affirmations (I am mentally strong), a list of achievement reminders (I won first place last time), and personal pep convos (I can do it) may increase mental toughness during lapses in self-confidence It is important to remember that self-talk is most effective when it is realistic. "I can win against this opponent because I have this pitch in my arsenal" is an example that is more effective than saying, "I will beat this person."

Focus

If you're looking for the quickest approach to unleash your potential to be mentally strong or self-disciplined, start with your capacity to concentrate. Without concentration, we are prone to deviating from anything or anybody that requires our attention. The lessons and exercises in this chapter emphasize the importance of safeguarding, expanding, and optimizing your capacity to concentrate.

One of the most significant impediments to having strong concentration is the lack of a clear sense of where you're headed. Take a minute before starting your next project to reflect on why you're doing it in the first place. Ask yourself the following questions:

1. What do I want to achieve?
2. What is my motivation for my actions?
3. Why is reading this book or this project important to me?
4. How will this project or book add meaning to my life?

When you do this exercise, you will know where you want to go and your work will proceed more smoothly.

Take a few minutes to describe how things will look and feel once you've reached your goal.

Concentration

You've probably heard the phrase "I must concentrate..." We all use this once in a while, even when it comes to simple things like eating, walking, driving, writing, and more serious duties like attempting to complete a significant project. The key to success is the power of concentration. Concentration helps revive our dormant energy and channels the power inside us to ease our road to better ideas and sucess. It is also an important aspect in mental toughness and self-discipline development.

When this skill is well developed, your mind obeys you quickly and does not follow meaningless ideas. Concentration is crucial in meditation, developing mental mastery, and achieving peace of mind. Without it, the mind just bounces from one notion to another. Do you have any ideas on how to improve it?

1. **Attention:** The state of your attention reflects brain activity. Attention is directly related to concentration and learning. If your attention is scattered and fragmented on numerous things and places, your brain

activity is likewise scattered and fragmented and you are unable to concentrate well and understand information easily.

2. **An Appropriate Environment:** Another crucial factor that determines concentration power is finding an appropriate environment, regardless of whether you are attempting to concentrate on your studies, employment, or any other task; the proper environment is a requirement if you want to concentrate well on your objective.

3. **Reading:** Reading is another really effective approach to improving your concentration. We're all guilty of reading something or the other. Many of us like reading a newspaper every day and maybe more are addicted to non-fiction, fiction novels, or worse, social media. The idea is to read a couple of pages from the newspaper or a book and then take up a pen and paper and write down whatever you have gained or learned from what you read.

Mental Toughness and the US Military

Here's an excellent illustration of mental toughness. Every year, around 1,300 cadets join the United States Military Academy, located at West Point. Cadets must complete a series of brutal exams during their first summer on campus. This summer initiation program is known all over the world as "Beast Barracks."

According to researchers who have discussed with West Point cadets, "Beast Barracks is deliberately constructed to test the very boundaries of cadets' physical, emotional, and mental capacities."

You would think that cadets who successfully complete Beast Barracks are larger, stronger, or tougher than their classmates. Angela Duckworth, a researcher at the University of Pennsylvania, found something different when she started tracking the cadets.

Duckworth's research uncovered how mental toughness, perseverance, and passion impact the ability to achieve goals. She tracked a total of 2,441 first year cadets at West Point. She recorded their high school ranks, scores, leadership potential score (which indicates participation in extracurricular activities), and physical aptitude exams (a standardized physical exercise evaluation).

Here's what she discovered. It wasn't a cadet's strength, intelligence, or leadership potential that accurately indicated whether or not he would complete Beast

Barracks. Instead, it was grit—the perseverance and passion to achieve long-term goals—that made the difference.

In fact, cadets with one standard deviation higher on the Grit Scale were 60% more likely than their peers to complete Beast Barracks. It was mental toughness, not talent, IQ, or genetics, that determined whether or not a cadet would be successful.

What is mental toughness for you?

Find out what mental toughness is for you. For the West Point Army cadets, mental toughness means finishing summer at Beast Barracks. For you it may be:

- One month without missing a workout
- One month without processed food
- Delivering work ahead of schedule
- Meditating every day
- Working out more than usual
- Calling a friend every Saturday
- Spending every evening doing something creative

Whatever it is, be clear about where you're heading. Mental toughness is an abstract quality, but in the real world, it is tied to concrete actions. You can't just think your way to being mentally strong; you have to prove it to yourself by accomplishing something of value to you in real life.

Chapter 5

Fear: The Destroyer of Your Persona, Self-Confidence, Self-Discipline, and Happiness

What exactly is fear? Is it positive or negative? Why is fear important, and what, if anything, does it have to do with blind people? Fear, at its most fundamental level, is a physical and emotional reaction to some external stimulus. Sometimes the stimulus is obvious—for example, a loud, unexpected crash in the middle of the night—but the trigger for fear is subconscious and difficult to trace.

Some aspects of fear are evolutionary; they are a hardwired set of autonomic responses that have been important to our survival, according to science (Ranchman, 1990). There is debate over the number of evolutionary fears, but two are often mentioned—fear of falling and fear of loud sounds. Evolutionary fears may be the root of other fears—consider, for example, fear of heights—but there are many fears that do now show proof of being hardwired into our brains.

Have you ever heard of escape rooms? Escape rooms are rooms in which people are locked in order to play a game that requires them to solve a series of puzzles in a certain amount of time in order to complete a goal, often obtaining the key to unlock the room. What have they got to do with fear?

When creating a dangerous escape game, escape room designers take a lot of factors into account. This includes the three fundamental types of fear: primal, irrational, and rational. Knowing the differences between these three types of fear is what makes or breaks a dangerous escape room.

Fear may be really powerful. Have you noticed? It causes us to doubt our abilities, suppress our creativity, and leave our dreams unfulfilled. If you ask me, living in fear is no way to live.

I've been studying fear for years, and here's what I've learned. You can't beat it, overtake it, ignore it, support it, or deny it (Ranchman, 1990). Push fear away or pretend it doesn't exist and all you get is more of its familiar effects, limitation, confusion, and disappointment in yourself. The only long-term, intelligent method to deal with fear is to take away its power.

How do you do that? By making fear your friend.

It may seem counterintuitive, but here's how it works. Resisting fear empowers it. Unseen fear creeps into your thoughts and takes control of your body. However, giving it your full, open, loving attention takes it out of the shadows.

Once you learn to recognize how fear drives your choices, you can choose differently by letting joy, enthusiasm, wholeness, and love into your life. This is how you kill fear and learn to live your life.

Familiarize yourself with fear in all of its manifestations. Make learning a way of life. Learn to see how it clouds your judgment and convinces you that you are not your intelligent, magnificent self.

Become an expert in your fear and it will lose its power over you. Make it your friend for life and your life will begin to sing its own unique and beautiful song.

Effects of Fear on the Body

Some of us come into the world predisposed to fear. You may have tension, anxiety, and inner agitation.

Make a practice of learning these bodily sensations. You'll be able to recognize fear as it begins to take hold. Focus on the sources of your fear, which are deep within you. Don't analyze or push them away. Simply feel and breathe, feel and breathe, feel and breathe.

Understand that these are only bodily sensations. There's no need to build a story around them or let them guide your decisions. Simply note them, then move on with living your beautiful life.

Exercise, do yoga, practice deep breathing, stroll in nature, and meditate to take good care of your fear-prone body. Be a kind host, even if fear is present. Know that a place of essential wholeness is inside you that has never been touched by fear and live from there.

Effects of Fear on the Mind

Fearful thoughts revolve around the word "no." They tell us we cannot, should not, and are not capable of something. They persuade us that if we express our true heart's desire, we will be judged, rejected, or abandoned. They make our heads whirl incessantly with worry. Do any of these ring a bell?

- I can't disappoint her/him.
- I might not succeed at this.
- I have doubts about doing this.
- I might feel overwhelmed.
- I will need to work hard.
- What happens if I get heavily criticized?
- What if things get more difficult?
- I do not know how to start doing this.
- I am so scared.

These ideas weave a familiar web, leaving you frustrated and unable to change. But this is not your true voice. This is simply fear speaking.

Here's how fear works. It makes you believe that it knows what the future holds and makes you expect only negative outcomes.

What is the truth about the future? You have no idea. You have no idea whether you will succeed or fail. But your fear-fueled mind convinces you that you will fail. And if you believe these thoughts, no wonder fear will paralyze you. What if what really happens is fantastic beyond your wildest dreams? What if you let yourself remain realistic, accept that you don't know what the future holds, and let life unfold naturally?

Why go one more second believing limited thoughts with bleak outcomes that aren't even true? Here's some medication for your fear-fueled thoughts:

- Pay attention to your mind so you can understand how it functions. Learn to recognize your own fear-driven thoughts.
- Take the prudent approach. Don't trust what your thoughts are saying. Recognize what is genuinely true:

you don't know what the future holds.

- Feel the liberation of being free of a bleak future that hasn't even occurred yet. Life is suddenly brimming with possibilities. Can you sense them?

Act

- You now understand how crucial it is to befriend your fear.
- You're aware of how fear manifests in your body.
- You can see how fear infiltrates your head.

This is the point at where the rubber meets the road. You have a choice. What do you really want now that you're no longer driven by fear? What do you want your life to be about?

Harness the power of fear by completely understanding it. Then locate your true voice - the one that is alive inside you and cannot be squelched no matter how much you believe in fear. When you're ready, get up and sing a note of your own wonderful song.

Fear is Our Teacher

Empowerment is the opposite of fear. Facing our fears is the most powerful method for us to learn about ourselves, develop from experience, and become a better, more empowered person. This was a core component of every young person's life in traditional societies, also known as initiation.

Ancient Europeans and many other nations lost their indigenous customs as a result of imperial invasion, which began with the Romans and continues to this day. Thankfully, there are still societies all over the globe that know that making fear a friend may result in deep change.

Fear is a bare mirror that reflects our deepest wounds, weaknesses, and shadows. However, every time you choose to face your fears, you are choosing to learn more about yourself and the world around you.

A Helpful Exercise

Instead of struggling with your ideas and stressing about whether they are good enough, make a commitment to yourself that you will no longer torture yourself.

Take a deep breath and then let your thoughts and words flow. To prepare yourself for overcoming your fear, remind yourself, "I am an outstanding _____," and fill in the blank with the role you are attempting to play.

For example, convince yourself, "I am an amazing writer," and then rush through the last few pages of your chapter. Repeat "I am" affirmations any time you feel the need to calm yourself.

Chapter 6

Daily Self-Discipline Tips

Following through with and completing the tasks we begin is a terrific approach to increase the potency of our self-discipline skills. When we leave a task incomplete, our minds remain in a state of tension even after we've moved on to other things to concentrate on. This phenomenon is connected with the Zeigarnik effect, named after psychologist Bluma Zeigarnik, who observed in 1927 that study participants who were given tasks and completed them performed twice as well as those who were not (Pashler, 2016).

Spending our leisure time worrying about what we haven't completed is seldom enjoyable or effective. Make it a habit to work step by step and be persistent until your task is finished. You'll discover how to avoid procrastination and fulfill your own drive to do the assignment.

Another strategy to improve our ability to complete our tasks is to get more comfortable with the concept of success. Many individuals confess to being terrified of success. To go boldly in that direction, we must perceive ourselves as worthy of achievement.

Though success often brings with it more responsibility and a heavier workload, it also enhances our capacity to deal with those changes. As you find more success, you are more driven to continue.

Your responsibility now is to hold on tight and believe that everything will be fine—and it will. You are adaptable, powerful, and resilient.

What do you do when you want to give up? This is the point in the self-discipline journey that we may choose to endure despite experiencing irritation and low energy. We can also choose to yield to the part of ourselves that doesn't feel capable enough to complete a task.

The fastest path to a happy ending here is to make it a habit to constantly encourage yourself. This habit may incorporate as many diverse tasks as you need to keep yourself focused on your objective.

It may be as simple as reminding yourself of the next actionable step, using a tracking sheet, listening to high-energy music, taking a small break, or speaking with someone who can cheer you up.

It doesn't matter how you encourage yourself so much as it does that you keep encouraging yourself. You'll leave space for procrastination if you don't put your heart into it. We can overcome procrastination and have the drive to see our endeavors through when we believe in ourselves.

First and foremost, you must prevent burnout. Burnout occurs when you are intellectually, emotionally, or physically exhausted. Burnout may occur when a constant stream of incoming demands is met without pauses or ways to eliminate stress. Burnout may occur even when we are doing something we like; in fact, burnout can occur when we begin missing meals or sleeping less in order to spend more time doing something we enjoy.

Fortunately, there are several strategies to prevent burnout. The most crucial suggestion is to build a consistent, everyday practice. Working at a steady pace prevents us from having to pull all-nighters or work under duress until the very last minute.

Another strategy to avoid burnout is to set reasonable goals for yourself. Understand that your energy, creativity, and production will have ups and downs. Avoid the need to push yourself incessantly to get things done. There's no need to fall into a productivity trap when you put in lots of effort but get nothing in return. Always be gentle to yourself and enjoy the improvements you're making along the way.

It is critical to ensure that you have enough free time. Give yourself genuine breaks on a regular basis to maintain your mind and body in good working order. Get outside—nature can be restorative and a welcome distraction from the work you do inside.

Another strategy to keep oneself healthy while working toward your goal is to recognize that although you may fail, you can turn failure into a great learning experience. What if you learned to see failure as only a signal to choose an alternative path forward? What if you determined that failure is just something that has to be worked out, reorganized, or reassessed, rather than an indication of your own weakness or failure?

We no longer have to be terrified of failing when we consider failure as something that may occur while making progress. Failure may be seen as an opportunity to try again, as well as a circumstance that may provide solutions for future success.

When your levels of self-discipline begin to wane, it may be time to start rewarding your efforts again. After you've performed the initial task, you may add prizes for achieving milestones, which are activities or accomplishments that must be achieved to unlock the ultimate goal. This will redirect your attention and motivate you to work harder. Make incentives that are unique or fascinating to you. The benefits might be physical, such as buying a new sweater, or intangible, such as the satisfaction of sticking to your fitness regimen five days in a row. For example, you might write a list of five methods to reward yourself for continuing to make improvements.

Now, I'd like to present to you some more useful examples, strategies, and tactics for developing self-discipline.

Technique 1: Spartan Self-Discipline

The Spartans were incredibly straightforward and disciplined. Their only purpose was to become fierce warriors and maintain Lycurgus' rules. Sparta got weak and finally faded away when they let the temptation of wealth, food, and luxury slip in.

Spartans had a few rules that they always followed:

- They had a simple life.
- They were against weakness and overindulgence.
- Wealth was not a concern.
- Character, merit, and discipline were of the utmost importance.
- Warfare and fitness were everything to them.
- Long hair was seen to be masculine.
- They were people of few words.

I've always liked the saying, "Don't pray for easy lives; rather, pray to be a stronger person." Take a moment and ask yourself:

- Have you ever prayed or wished to become more powerful?
- Have you ever prayed or wished to be safe or protected?

Your answer to both questions is likely yes. Now, think about this. What if instead, you prayed regularly to become more resilient, stronger, and more disciplined? What would happen then? I know the answer. People would be thrust into situations in which they would need to be stronger, more resilient, and more disciplined. That is quite interesting. This made me rethink discipline. So I started researching it from this perspective.

The Spartan Way of Life

The Spartans were unrivaled in terms of discipline. Everything they did was motivated by a single goal: to be the best warriors possible. They excelled in just one thing, which was warfare.

They grew so focused on this that they lost sight of the necessity for anything else. Lycurgus, who is known as Sparta's father, crafted a system of rules. In this system, money was made of wood and land was split among all people, so that merit and character were valued more than money.

According to Aristotle, freedom comes with discipline. Every individual in the world desires freedom, particularly those who have permanent life responsibilities such as spouses, children, and parents and those whose jobs are devoid of meaning.

The work itself isn't always devoid of meaning. However, there are many expenses that the work is supposed to provide for, including:

- Car payments
- Mortgage payments
- Eating out
- Buying things

Those things do not provide freedom but they need to be covered. Instead, as your income grows, so do your possessions. This does not equal more freedom, however. Here's an example from the Spartans:

Once upon a time, a man (Spartans were focused on males rather than females) was astounded by how modest King Agesilaus' and all Spartans' clothes and meals were. "Freedom is what we receive from this way of life, my friend," King Agesilaus said. Discipline is built through time through the choices that a person makes; it does not begin in the womb. Consider all of the decisions you've already made today:

- The choice of waking up to the alarm or hitting the snooze button.
- The choice of eating a healthy breakfast or merely cereal or a pop tart.
- The choice to exercise or not to exercise.
- The choice to browse social media or work on a project.

Discipline may be seen as a sequence of decisions. The more proficient you grow at making decisions, the more disciplined and liberated you will become.

The Simple Spartan Discipline

Spartans were famous for their simple statements. Sparta was known as Lacedaemon, from which the term "laconic" comes.

A laconic phrase, also known as laconism, is a short or concise remark, particularly an elliptical and blunt rejoinder. It is called after Laconia, a region of Greece that includes the city of Sparta, whose ancient people were known for their linguistic austerity and for their blunt and sometimes snappy comments.

Philip II of Macedon is a noteworthy example. He shifted his attention to Sparta after capturing southern Greece and obtaining the surrender of other significant city-states. He questioned menacingly whether he should approach as a friend or adversary. "Neither," was the response. "You are urged to surrender without further delay because if I send my army into your territory, I will burn your fields, slaughter your people, and raze your city," he said, losing patience. The Spartan ephors responded once again with a single word: If. As a result, neither Philip nor his son Alexander the Great tried to take the city.

Speaking was essential in Sparta. If you did not speak up, then you were not worth it at all. This kind of terseness appeals to me and it is most noticeable in those who have a clear sense of purpose and discipline. At the end of the day, character, honesty, merit, and hard work are valued more than being well-dressed, having the latest phone, or posting the best pictures on Instagram.

Learn to talk less while doing more because:

- Doing > Talking
- Freedom > Stuff

The Spartan way of life suggests:

Simplifying your life.

Spartans were indifferent to money or possessions. Instead, they were concerned with freedom, even if it meant dying for it. It was essential to preserve their laws and discipline.

Most people nowadays have no moral compass or stance. Instead, they give in to everything they fancy and bend to every whim. Mass consumption is corruptible in the same way that leprosy is. If a person is unable to abstain from what they want, they will constantly be playing a losing game.

This is terrible. If there are 12 people in a room and you put 12 cookies on the table and warn them not to eat them, a few will eat one and persuade others to eat theirs as well. In the end, there is always going to be one person that won't eat one and another one who will eat two cookies.

The person who chooses to not have one has control over themselves. Others may believe they have power, but they do not. Real power is having control over your earthly fleeting desires. Make your life easier. Get rid of what you don't need and learn to live with less.

Becoming physically fit.

The Spartans were well-known for their commitment to physical fitness. After all, they were supposed to be lifetime warriors and we were forbidden from pursuing any other occupation except that of a fighter in the military.

You must be physically fit, much like the Spartans were. That way, you will learn how to become disciplined. Spartans didn't simply work out; they trained constantly.

Technique 2: Navy SEAL Self-Discipline

This elite group of soldiers is focused on achieving success in difficult and unexpected terrain. They see their suffering as a source of joy. They emphasize resilience and proficiency in order to become invincible. On the path to success, you must concentrate on aspects that might propel you to success and you must redefine yourself. Elite Navy members simplify their lives and train like Spartans did, and they also:

Don't quit.

"I will not quit," states the Navy SEAL creed. "In the face of hardship, I persevere and thrive. I will get back up if I am knocked down every single time. I'm never out of a battle." There will be many problems and barriers in life. This sometimes necessitates venturing into seas that you are unfamiliar with. Persistence and dedication will propel you past these obstacles.

Pay close attention to everything they learn.

Focus on your prior experiences and use them to your advantage, whether it's a mistake you've made in the past or something a mentor has taught you. Leadership is taught and learned in the Navy SEAL. To be successful in life, you must learn to make adjustments along the way. You must be versatile, move quickly, and learn from past success.

Relate well to others.

Self-discipline is fundamental to living a good, meaningful life. Making choices in life based purely on what we do and do not want to do will not get us very far. It would be chaos. If you study the lives of phenomenally successful people—from athletes to novelists to entrepreneurs—you will notice one consistent theme: self-discipline. Every day, regardless of the circumstances, they would do what is necessary to go ahead. They don't do it because they want to. They don't do it because it is convenient for them. They don't always do it after a nice night's sleep or because the mood strikes. They work hard every day, no matter what.

Destroy the opponents.

You learn from the Navy SEALs that you have to accept competition. On the path to success, there will always be competition. Communicate well with your team and concentrate on reducing how to best counter it.

Everyday Tips

To remain on course, pay attention to the right cues.

Determine which cues will help you maintain your self-control on a daily basis after answering the carrot or stick question. Having three hyper-productive days in a row has always been a challenge for me. I'll go two days without procrastinating, then on the third, the master procrastinator in my head takes control.

I usually leave visual cues on my desk at the end of my last productive day since I am more of a carrot person. If I have to complete an assignment, I'll leave out some of my previous work. This way, I'm happy to remind myself of the benefits of self-discipline.

In the same manner, I use clues that emphasize the link between short-term self-discipline and long-term achievement. Journal excerpts, for example, might indicate many hours of hard work right next to the paychecks that I received many months of hard work. Find methods to remind yourself of the power of everyday self-control, regardless of how you do it. The more reminders you have, the less likely you are to procrastinate and be lazy.

Accountability is a critical component of self-discipline.

You must be responsible not just to others but also to yourself.

When it comes to personal responsibility, attempt to keep a journal of your journey and monitor your progress as often as possible. Write a few phrases in your journal every night if you want to improve your self-discipline. Include the good, the terrible, and the ugly of your current situation, and don't keep anything from yourself.

In the long term, you'll realize that self-mastery is nothing more than a collection of days in which you came closer to your objectives because of personal responsibility.

Aside from journaling, seeking assistance from your peers is also crucial. If you struggle with self-discipline, it helps to talk with someone who inspires you to stay the course, such as a spouse or a friend.

Final Words

It's been a long road through this book, and if you're still here, congrats on sticking with it. You've taken a few more steps down the hard road of self-discipline. We've looked at what self-discipline is, how it works, and how you can adapt it to benefit your life.

Those skills begin with changing your fundamental beliefs and self-beliefs like I also did many years ago. You need a mental image of the person you wish to be and reinforce it through smaller choices. For me, it began with morning rituals at university and progressed from there. I learned to chunk tasks, to work hard days with a lesser output if necessary, and to make daily schedules.

Since then, I've started to plan my life, regulate my thoughts and emotions, and promote my growth by adopting a better lifestyle that includes a healthy diet, exercise, relaxation, and socializing. Going beyond one's comfort zone in several aspects of life has also been beneficial. You may gain a lot from pushing your limits in general.

Most of us seek a moderate level of success, just enough to live our lives. It's about living a happy life, and most people don't want to be Elon Musk. They do not want to live to work. Most individuals want to enjoy themselves, which is just fine. I don't need billions to be happy.

Remember, this is a long-distance marathon, not a sprint. To be in it for the long haul, you must gradually adjust so as not to overburden yourself.

Exercise self-control and begin to break old, harmful behaviors. Again, take it gently if necessary. Don't overburden yourself. Your body and mind are key components of the machine that is you, and you need them to function efficiently in order to have the greatest chance of success.

Best wishes on your journey to self-discipline. I hope these strategies will help you. Now that you've reached this point, you're ready to start, but not before learning the best time management techniques.

So turn the page and let us get started!

***

"Don't be fooled by the calendar. There are only as many days in the year as you make use of. One man gets only a week's value out of a year while another man gets a full year's value out of a week."

- Charles Richards

Introduction

Time Management

I was never one of those people that stressed over time but the need to increase the level of effectiveness in my career and personal life made me start paying attention to it. One day, I decided to improve my career level and prove to my boss that I am worthy of promotion. As you already presume, I requested far more projects than I usually take on monthly.

But as they say, before you eat the elephant make sure you know what parts you want to eat. I did not pay attention to the projects, or to be more specific, their requirements, importance, or duration. I just took them on and promised my boss that I will figure everything out at the end of the month. Guess what? I did not deliver a single project and I obviously only informed my team about it at the last minute. That caused additional stress not only to me but to them and to my management as well. And all this happened because I failed to manage my time well.

You see, time waits for no one—that is the hard truth. It is the only resource that people can't buy, borrow, or barter. Time also does not follow one of the main tenets of the law of supply and demand, namely, the idea that when the demand goes up to a high level, the supply will increase to meet it. Humans may use different amounts of time to accomplish tasks, results, and goals but everyone is given the same amount of time each day—24 hours or 86,400 seconds.

Over time, the behaviors that I exhibited, and that you probably have at times as well, are sure to cause resentment. This can result in repeated conflicts in the workplace, and at home. After all, poor time management causes stress. Stress affects our health and emotions and results in low mood and lack of motivation that additionally prevent managing time successfully. I tried to complete my projects at the last minute because I did not effectively manage my time. I sat and relaxed in front of the television without doing work, I was constantly scrolling through social media, and I waited until the end of the month to finish the projects I took on voluntarily. I sacrificed the quality of my work, I missed my deadlines, I caused stress, and I impacted others negatively.

Of course, I did not get a promotion. What I did get, however, was awareness. Awareness of a problem that I had subconsciously—my inability to manage time. I never paid attention to something that could make my future better. I realized that time is one of the top reasons for success or failure in my life. Investing bigger amounts of time into a goal, objective, need, or even weakness can tip the balance of success in my favor.

After learning how to manage time, I started achieving my goals way faster than before. I started with fixing the damage I had done in my workplace and I finally got the long-awaited promotion. I started being effective, I did not multitask anymore, and I focused on one activity at a time for a specified duration. I did more in less time by prioritizing essential tasks that require immediate action and by creating a proper schedule.

I wrote this book because I had walked in your shoes for quite a while and I know the pain that you are experiencing at the moment. How are you going to solve your problem with time management? You should do it the same way I did.

I am going to show you exactly how to manage your time. In this book, I will first explain time, its management, and its importance. Then, I will show you the negative side of procrastinating, of using a smartphone improperly, and how to get over them with the help of concentration and motivation. Finally, I will introduce you to some of the most important time management principles and techniques, like the Pareto and the Pomodoro principles, and I will end this book with some everyday tips.

I want you to know that I am going to walk you through, step-by-step, until you learn how to manage time. You see, this is not just theory; it consists of real techniques, tools, and strategies that I have personally used, coached, taught, and researched. They help you with your discipline, goals, values, habits, management styles, and persuasion. I've seen them bring forth a bounty of results in my life as well as in the lives of countless others.

As stated above, for a long amount of time, I was in your shoes. I had no idea about the importance of time management and the benefits that can result from it. I was stuck and I was not able to go forward in either my professional or my private life. I was suffering and I knew that I had to make a change. I am grateful for that change and I am proud of myself because I have been applying my time management skills for over 15 years now. They work and they deliver results.

Are you ready to learn about time management and the skills required for successfully implementing it into your life? If your answer is yes, keep reading.

Chapter 7

Time Management: What Does It Mean?

The 84,400 seconds per day we get may seem a lot but they go fast. Regardless of how quickly time seems to fly by for you, even the most skilled time manager's hours, minutes, and seconds tick by at the same rate. How do you perceive time? Do most of the things that you do daily feel mechanical and not personally gratifying?

People constantly look at other people and realize that quite a few of them get a lot more done than they do. That is not happening because they have more time but because of their time management skills. Without a doubt, managing your time will positively affect your goals and, in the end, your success.

Time is the substance of our lives. We don't create time in our lives but instead "create our lives in time." But people too often feel that, in their personal and professional lives, time is running them. They feel they only have time for one life—personal or professional—but not both. The difference in giving your time more meaning or making it more productive is not found in trying to speed up or slow down your days. It is what you choose to do within the time frames that constrain you that makes the difference (Cross, 1980).

Answer this for me—are you taking advantage of the time that is available to you? Some people seem to have been born with a natural understanding of time management. Fortunately for the rest of us, it's a skill that can be learned and developed.

"Time management" can be defined as the process of oganizing and planning how to split your time between activities. If you become good at time management, you will become able to work smarter, not harder. Learning these skills will make you able to work smarter and not harder and you will do a lot more things than before in less time. Yes, this will be the case even when your activities will be abundant and you'll experience pressure and short deadlines.

The people I mentioned above, the most skilled time managers, are able to manage their time extremely well. They use different time-management techniques that are included in this book because they improve a person's ability to function more effectively.

Let me put it like this. Senior executives and CEOs seem to possess unique time management and organization skills that enable them to dramatically increase their productivity. Indeed, people who are good at managing their time have strong skills in several key areas. They have a clear vision of their big-picture goals at work and in life —long-term, yearly, monthly, weekly, and daily goals. They are skillful at breaking these goals down into smaller units, and they know how to translate these small units into action-oriented to-do lists filled with tasks. Finally, they understand that achieving long- and medium-range goals means crossing off every task they can on their to-do list, every day.

Ultimately, how well you manage time boils down to your level of personal motivation. How willing are you to learn from the mistakes you've made about using time in the past? How willing are you to go after the things you know are important to do for the future? Most people know what needs to be done; they even know how to do it. They just don't have their priorities straight at the moment they make decisions about how to spend their time. Being more efficient in the present will help you achieve the future of your dreams. First, however, you need to motivate yourself to change some of your thinking and your habits (Cross, 1980).

To explain the previous sentence better I will include an example. I will dedicate this paragraph to the first real person included in this book, Benjamin Franklin.

Benjamin Franklin was a successful author, politician, scientist, philosopher, printer, inventor, activist, and diplomat. His accomplishments are astounding. He was a scientist known for his theories and discoveries and gained the recognition of fellow scientists and intellectuals. He was a political writer and activist and served as a diplomat during the American Revolutionary War. He was a newspaper editor and self-published author. Franklin started the first American library. His achievements go on and on. Benjamin Franklin is even credited for the statement, "Time is money." How did he find the time to do all this?

The good news is there is no more time! How can that be good news?

- In this respect, the playing field is level.
- Everyone gets the same twenty-four hours in a day.
- Your competition has no more hours in a day than you.
- The richest man cannot buy even one more minute of time in a day!
- You can only manage yourself and your own activities more effectively.

In a typical forty-hour workweek, it's estimated that the average person spends:

- 1.7 hours looking for things
- 1 hour rescheduling appointments and tasks

- 1.4 hours wasted because of rescheduled appointments and tasks
- 2.2 hours wasted because of lack of organization and priorities

This is a total of more than 6 hours wasted due to poor planning and a lack of organization. When people are asked why they are not organized, the number one reason given is:

"I don't have the time."

The fact is people choose to be disorganized. Most people could save this wasted time by spending just two hours a week organizing and planning. In just two hours of planning, you could free an additional three to four hours of prime time every week.

This book is about behavioral changes. Learning how to spend more time acting instead of reacting. The skills described herein will help you become better organized and manage time more effectively, which will increase your productivity if you adopt the behavioral changes outlined throughout this book.

Chapter 8

Managing Time and Goals

IN ONE SENSE, TIME management is about managing your goals. If you know what you want to achieve in the future, you can figure out how to use your time in order to get there.

These are the three elements of goal management:

- **Long-term goals**—These are the goals toward which you direct your efforts. Typically, long-term goals are completed in a year or more.

- **Objectives**—These are the steps needed to achieve a long-term goal. Objectives are typically completed in a month or more.
- **Tasks**—These are the series of daily and weekly actions required to meet your objectives.

To help you get the right things done—that is, get where you want to go at work and in life—it's important to line up your daily actions and your long-term goals. Thus, the first step is setting the right long-term goals and then making sure your objectives and daily actions support those goals.

Goals: Their Importance and How To Set Them

A goal is a purpose toward which you direct your endeavors. For example, your goal could be to increase your company's sales revenue by 15%. A soccer team's goal might be to win the yearly championship. A student's goal might be to earn an MBA degree.

There's an art to setting goals. The most effective goals are specific and measurable and should be motivating. If a goal is too vague—for example, the resolution to make your firm the "best company in the world"—you will not be able to monitor your progress toward that goal, or even know whether or not you have achieved it. Does being the "best company in the world" mean "greatest sales" or "a greater return on sales" than any other company? Does it mean that your employee retention rate is the highest of the firms in your field? If the goal you articulate can't be measured, take another stab at defining it (Eccles, Wigfield, 2002).

An effective goal is also ambitious but not impossible to achieve. For instance, a goal of earning an MBA within six months is not realistic; getting the degree within two or three years is reasonable, on the other hand. Assigning a reasonable amount of time for the completion of your goals is essential. Only if you've established a clear and realistic deadline will you be able to determine how to best accomplish a goal. How you define a long-term goal is, to some degree, up to you. Is it a goal you want to achieve in the long term or the short term?

Regardless of what that timeframe is, strong time managers break down their long-term goals into objectives. If your long-term goal is to finish a particularly complex project within a year, for example, your objectives will state what you need to do in the next month, the next three months, the next six months, and so on to meet your long-term goal.

To move toward achieving these objectives, effective time managers break these objectives down further into tasks—things that you need to do in the short term—within the week, the day, or the hour. This process of dividing a long-term goal into smaller segments is also known as chunking. Look at a goal as you would a big bar of chocolate. It's just not possible to stuff the whole thing in your mouth at once, even if that's your first impulse. So, you break it into pieces. First, you divide it into halves or quarters, and then you break it apart further into individual squares. Most people eat the chocolate bar a square at a time—and it doesn't take long for the whole bar to disappear (Eccles, Wigfield, 2002).

The most important thing to remember is not to obsess about your long-term goal, although you can think about it, discuss it as appropriate, and perhaps jot down notes to yourself about it on occasion. This will help you remember the direction in which you're headed as you focus on the chunks that you have determined will take you there. Keeping your ultimate goal at the back of your mind makes you understand the chunks you're doing at any moment and gives them more meaning than they might otherwise have.

Remain focused on implementation and action. Achieve your tasks and objectives, and you'll hit the big target right where and when you're supposed to. As long as your goal setting achieves the proper traction, you'll reach your destination, no matter how far down the road it is. When working toward your goals, remember the Eastern proverb that wisely state that "a journey of a thousand miles begins with a single step."

Dos and Don'ts

It's important to keep your energy and motivation high when you're trying to improve your time-management skills.

To avoid losing momentum, consider the following:

- Do write down your goals and post them in a visible spot where you'll see them regularly.

- Do remember what you ultimately hope to achieve. Keep your eye on the prize, so to speak.

- Don't forget why you're doing what you're doing.

- Do work with a teammate who will keep you honest about your progress and compliment you on your efforts.

- Do celebrate and reward yourself when you meet objectives and accomplish goals.

Priorities: Define and Organize Them

In our complex world, you can't wait until you have reached one long-term goal before moving on to the next. On any given day, you will be working on short-term tasks associated with multiple long-term goals and objectives. So how do you decide which to do first? You prioritize them.

But how do you decide which tasks take priority over others? Which tasks should be completed first, second, third, and so forth?

The first step is to have a clear understanding of what's involved in each task by asking the following questions—who, what, when, where, why, and how.

- **Who?** Who needs this to be done—your boss, a customer, a coworker, or a subordinate? Who will be performing the task? Who will benefit from this? Does the person asking you to do this task understand the demands it will make on your time and energy?

- **What?** What exactly are you required to do? Is it valuable to the big picture? Does the benefit of doing the job justify the investment of your time, energy, and resources?

- **When?** By what date do you need to complete your task? Do you have the time to accommodate this request? Former president Dwight D. Eisenhower explained that truly important things are rarely urgent and urgent things are rarely important. Unimportant things usually become urgent because of poor planning. Keep your priorities in mind as you take on new work.

- **Where?** Are there any geographic differences that will have an impact on the timelines of the task you've been assigned? Are there time-zone differences, for example, that will need to be taken in consideration? If you are working with someone in a different office, state, or country, do you need to consider the time it will take to send communications or documents back and forth between those two locations?

- **Why?** Why have you been asked to complete this task? Why is it necessary in the context of long-term goals? Understanding the big picture will help you stay focused and prioritize better.

- **How?** How should you complete the task? How will your completed task be measured or evaluated? The way that something needs to be done has a huge effect on time management decisions and on the quality and cost of the task.

Dos and Don'ts

If you are having trouble dealing with your workload in a reasonable amount of time, it might be time to consider these tips. Followed routinely, they will make a seemingly endless list of tasks more doable.

- Do ask yourself the basic questions outlined above.

- Do make lists and stick to them. According to experts, lists are one of the most effective time management tools.

- Do allow yourself more time than you think you need to perform the tasks you need to do. Don't let distraction sabotage your list of tasks.

- Don't forget to factor in time sinks like sending emails and returning phone calls.

- Don't fall into time traps like playing games on your phone or browsing online.

A Schedule: Create and Implement It

The second step? Creating and implementing a schedule. While some people are highly organized, many people are drawn into chaos by the demands of their work and of others. In fact, they are so habitually disorganized and stressed that they feel they cannot invest the time necessary to bring order to their lives, no matter what they do.

But organizing yourself and your time is not as difficult as it seems. This is done with the help of scheduling. Additionally, it will eliminate a great deal of stress. Scheduling involves creating systems that are consistent ways of doing things. Systems transform your daily, weekly, monthly, and yearly goals, objectives, and tasks into a coordinated whole (Cross, 1980).

For many working professionals, a day is an exercise in playing catch-up. You may be late for your ten o'clock meeting because you had to respond to an urgent email. The meeting itself runs too long. A crisis with a client interrupts lunch. Before you know it, three o'clock rolls around and you are just barely getting started with the tasks that need to get done that day. The secret to avoiding chaotic days such as this one is effective scheduling.

Not many of us know that there are many ways to look at time. Here is an exercise that will help you discover which time is more important to you.

Which of these are most important to you?

- Work time is time allotted to earning money.
- Self-time recharges your batteries and restores your physical, spiritual, and emotional well-being.
- Family time allows you to build and sustain relationships with the most important people in your life.
- Relationship time involves other people who matter to you—old and new friends, colleagues, schoolmates, and neighbors.
- Financial time goes to financial planning, investing, budgeting, dealing with bills and taxes, and so on.
- Community time is spent improving your community whether by volunteering at church or building a community garden.
- Education time is devoted to learning by taking classes, watching documentaries, reading, or studying online.

You might have other ways to look at time that are important to you, such as hobby time, exercise time, or travel time. Whatever they might be, understanding the different ways to look at time will help you manage it and balance your life more effectively.

Scheduling is all about being prepared. Most problems or crises you face on a daily basis are rarely that much of a surprise. You probably have encountered them before. That weekly ten o'clock meeting at work always runs late and that particular client always threatens to go to your competitor after receiving the first quotation for a project. Proper scheduling takes into account all your on-the-job knowledge and experience to prevent expected—and unexpected—problems from knocking you flat.

A good schedule is flexible enough to accommodate unforeseen developments and complications that can be anticipated. It should never push the agenda off track. A good scheduler always has a plan B. Creating a schedule that anticipates all possible SNAFUs is critical.

The first step to creating a sound schedule is assessing your to-do list. If you've ranked the items on your to-do list according to their importance, then you'll have a clear idea of what tasks absolutely need to get done on any given week. At the beginning of the week, take a look at your to-do list and estimate how long it will take you to complete each task. If you aren't good at figuring out how much time is needed to do various tasks, start keeping track of how long it takes you to complete each task, including any interruptions, and make a note to yourself for the future (Cross, 1980).

Once you've determined how long each task will take, plan the time when you will tackle them. Decide which day you will do item number one, number two, and so on, and plug the tasks into a daily planner or online calendar. Don't implement as many tasks as possible on the first day of the week. Instead, distribute the tasks evenly throughout the week, taking into consideration already scheduled meetings and deadlines for tasks.

Be sure to factor some extra time in the day to complete daily activities, such as responding to emails and returning phone calls.

Always allow more time to complete each task than you've estimated. If you think a project will take an hour, give yourself an hour and 15 minutes or even an hour and a half. Remember that it doesn't take a crisis to gobble up time unexpectedly. Activities you forget to include in your schedule will wipe out what you thought was extra time every day.

Dos and Don'ts

When you begin to make a detailed schedule, it is good to be aware of any pitfalls that may be lurking in the shadows. A good schedule is always prepared for and ready to accommodate surprises.

- Do be prepared for crises and unexpected events. Schedule time for them.
- Don't forget to be flexible.
- Don't neglect to have a plan B in case of unforeseen emergencies.
- Do assess your to-do list according to the importance of each task.
- Do become aware of how much time you need to complete certain tasks. This will help you better manage the time that you have.
- Don't try to get it all done in one day; instead, spread specific tasks over the course of a week.
- Do schedule time for thinking—a vital part of getting the work done.

Chapter 9

Stop Procrastinating by Concentrating

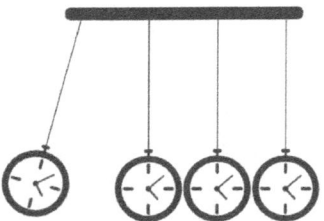

"Procrastination" is derived from the Latin verb procrastinare—to put off a task until tomorrow. But it's more than just voluntarily delaying. Procrastination is also derived from the ancient Greek word akrasia—doing something against our better judgment. It is a self-harming action towards the self.

If you're a procrastinator, then you've probably asked yourself at some point, "why do I procrastinate so much?" or "why do I keep procrastinating even though I know that it's bad for me?" These are important questions, since understanding why you procrastinate is crucial if you want to figure out how to stop doing it (Aquila, 1992).

Procrastination: Why It Happens

Although people talk about procrastination a lot, there can be considerable differences in what they mean by the term. Psychologists who study this topic make an important distinction: procrastination is a form of delay, but not every type of delay is procrastination. Before working on ways to reduce your procrastination, it's useful to understand this distinction and recognize times when you're delaying a task but not actually procrastinating (O'Donoghue, Rabin, 2001). For instance, you might need to delay some activities due to sudden changes in your situation or because you simply can't get everything done at the same time. So you might delay an activity to suit your schedule better. Although these instances involve putting off something, psychologists would not consider them procrastination.

Another particularly important distinction to make is between strategic delay and procrastination. The two are often confused. Strategic delay entails deliberately putting off a task as a way to generate time pressure as a source of motivation. Many people defend this strategy, saying it works for them, and some even claim it's the only way they can accomplish things. By putting pressure on themselves, they feel stimulated to work harder. However, it's a risky strategy because you might run out of time. It also consumes a lot of energy and can lead to a dip in which you feel exhausted after a deadline. What's more, there isn't much evidence to suggest it works by comparison to following a plan that is more balanced.

Procrastination is arguably even more irrational than strategic delay because the person will often be fully aware that delaying a task will have negative consequences, yet they still choose to delay. This is puzzling from a psychological perspective. For instance, even if someone has intended many times to finally file their taxes and they fully recognise it would be in their best interest to do so, they still don't do it. Instead, they start to watch their favorite TV series, perhaps thinking that they might feel more like it after one episode. But when the next episode is suggested, they start watching it. After that, they think to themselves, "It is really too late to start on the taxes now. Tomorrow I will feel more like it." and then they go to bed. Procrastination describes this type of delay, where there is a striking gap or mismatch between your intention and the actual action you take and you feel incapable of overcoming it.

The psychological explanation for this common but irrational behavior is that, by avoiding the emotional discomfort of engaging in the behavior, procrastination provides temporary relief or an escape. The task might go undone, but at least the confrontation with the negative emotion is avoided (O'Donoghue, Rabin, 2001). Easier and more fun things encourage us to stay away, at least momentarily, from what needs to be done. This is the main problem: procrastination is avoidance behavior. It is the avoidance of something aversive by occupying your thoughts with something you would rather do that is available right now, not in the future. It can be seen as a conflict between what you want to do now versus what you should be doing for your future self. In short, it is a self-regulation problem.

Of course, at different times, some people might use both strategic delay and procrastination, depending on the particular activity. The key difference between them is the emotional connotations—that is, putting pressure on oneself purposefully versus irrational avoidance that runs counter to one's intentions (O'Donoghue, Rabin, 2001).

A common idea about procrastination is that it is triggered by fear of failure but we know that it is not just fear that leads to procrastination. Anything aversive can trigger it—boredom, resentment, difficulty, disgust, practically anything that is negative in your mind. Almost everyone has experienced needing to do something they would rather avoid.

What Are You Avoiding?

We are not always consciously aware of our emotions. You could use your journal to focus on when exactly you feel bad. Perhaps you'll see a pattern in the types of tasks and obligations that are likely to make you procrastinate. If you recognize a pattern, it might be possible to do something pragmatic about it. For example, it might be possible to delegate the obligation you inherited to someone else, organise activities differently, or have others step in to help you. Rather than avoiding it, perhaps you can find a practical solution to have the activity happen.

Once you get started, it can be helpful to manage your emotional discomfort by making the task more pleasurable, reminding yourself of its ultimate purpose and making it less arduous.

Learn Why Concentration Is Important

Concentration is the ability to direct one's attention at will. Concentration means control of attention. It is the ability to focus the mind on one subject, object, or thought and, at the same time, exclude from the mind every other unrelated thought, idea, feeling, or sensation. That last part is the tricky part for most of us (Howland, 2007). To concentrate is to exclude or not pay attention to every other unrelated thought, idea, feeling, or sensation. It refers to ignoring what is going on around us, the smartphone making the sound that indicates that we received a text or email, or the open tabs on our computer as we work.

Frequent distractions affect productivity. It takes longer to finish a task when you're not concentrating. You can't focus on listening. You don't comprehend things as well and end up misunderstanding, misinterpretating, and creating conflict. It affects memory. You forget things or can't recall information promptly, which affects your personal life and your professional image.

Factors that affect concentration in people include:
- Distraction
- Insufficient sleep
- Insufficient physical activity
- Bad eating habits
- Environment

All of these elements can affect your concentration. Happily, they are also all addressable.

If you frequently can't focus your thoughts and are experiencing ongoing concentration difficulties, this may indicate a cognitive, medical, psychological, lifestyle, or environmental cause. Depending on the cause, you may have to temporarily accept that your concentration is low and learn a few tricks to reduce its impact or accept the dips as they come.

First, you need to eliminate distractions. How do we focus better if we are always bombarded with information? Make a practice to block time in your schedule to do specific tasks or activities. During this time, request that you be left alone or go to a place where others are unlikely to disturb you, like a library, a coffee shop, or a private room.

Second, reduce multitasking because it is not beneficial at all. Attempting to perform multiple activities at the same time makes us feel productive. It's also a recipe for lower focus, poor concentration, and lower productivity. Lower productivity can lead to burnout. Examples of multitasking include listening to a podcast while responding to an email or talking to someone over the phone while writing a report. Such multitasking not only hampers your ability to focus but compromises your work quality.

Third, focus on the moment. It might feel counterintuitive when you feel unable to concentrate, but remember that you choose what you focus on. It's tough to concentrate when your mind is always in the past or worrying about the future. While it isn't easy, make an effort to let go of past events. Acknowledge their impact, what you felt, and what you learned from them, then let them go.

Last but not least, switch tasks. While we may want to concentrate on a particular task, sometimes we get stuck and our brain needs something fresh to focus on. Try switching to other tasks or something you love to do. Switching tasks can help you stay alert and productive for a longer period.

With strong concentration skills, you will start using every second of the day. I am ending this chapter with one simple exercise for concentration.

"Count the words in any one paragraph in a book or newspaper and then count them again to ascertain that you have counted them correctly. Practice this exercise every day for several times. When this becomes easy, try counting the words in two paragraphs, and later, count the words on a whole page. To enhance your focus and attention, count the words mentally, only with your eyes, without pointing your finger at them."

Chapter 10

The Influence of Your Smartphone

TODAY, WHEN THE WORLD is globalized and fast-moving, it is impossible for humans to imagine their day-to-day activities without smartphones. They may be one of the most successful  inventions ever and have become a convenient means of communication. Today's smartphones are able to perform many other functions as well; they serve as music players, organizers, cameras, search engines, etc. Believe it or not, there are almost 6 billion cell phone users in the world (Kushlev, Leitao, 2020). I do not find anything strange here because people need phones in all spheres of their lives

—private and professional. However, if you ask me, smartphones are able to influence us negatively when it comes to time management. To be more specific, their excessive use is responsible for this issue.

There are certain harmful effects that are definitely caused by the overuse of smartphones. If you take a look at a few research articles, you learn that they may cause decreased attention, shortness of temper, sleep disorders, depression, headaches, and waste.

However, it is wrong to say that smartphones only harm us and waste our time. But I will focus on the negative side before I shift to the positive side of their use.

"Smartphones waste people's time." I do not have a problem with this sentence because this sentence is partly true. To explain it better, the times you check out your phone add up to an average of 90 minutes of phone time per day. In a year, that daily time adds up to 23 days and over your lifetime it becomes 3.9 years. Let's not forget that smartphones evolve all the time. They become more functional, and as expected, these numbers are going to become higher as time passes.

The question is: what are people doing on their smartphones during these 90 minutes, 23 days, and 3.9 years? Sadly, a lot of them are wasting their time. Do you wonder why? Well, the most used app category is social media, which makes up 14% of smartphone use time. TV, video apps, and telecom apps come in second at 9%. Communication apps come in third at 7%. Music, maps, and gaming apps come next. This means that for most people, smartphones turn into the ultimate time wasters (Kushlev, Leitao, 2020).

Smartphones' primary downside is their addictive nature (Kushlev, Leitao, 2020). A few years back, I became so addicted to texting that I decided to give it up—first for a short period of time and then forever. I decided to call people if I wanted to ask them something or to speak to them. I started to make plans to see them in real life without texting them. That is when I realized that nothing could replace face-to-face communication.

If you focus more on the topic, smartphones are addictive mostly because they are always within arm's reach. We should continue to enjoy our digital connection. However, our real lives are more important. Just like with anything else, too much of a good thing may not be a good thing after all.

Also, smartphones are likely to encourage mental laziness. Mental laziness is not a good trait when it comes to time management. Smartphones encourage mental laziness when, instead of doing math in your head or with pen and paper—say, when you're splitting a restaurant bill with friends—you may just use your phone's calculator instead.

How to Stop Wasting Time on Smartphones?

I am going to start this section with social media. As I told you before, social media applications on our phones are the most used of all apps and they are also the biggest time-waster when it comes to time. I am not going to lie to you, they are my favorite when it comes to keeping in touch with friends and family. I also use them to read blogs. But I was not like this. Before I realized the importance of time, I spent way too much time scrolling on Instagram and Facebook instead of working. Keep your social media applications out of sight so they are out of your mind. This is how I did it. I left my phone outside the room I was working in and I gave myself a few times each day to check my phone. I also tracked my time online. If you find yourself reaching for your phone every time it alerts you of a notification, change your notification settings. Restrict notifications while you are doing something important. Positive reinforcement is something that I have implemented on this journey as well. To be more specific, I set up a reward system—no social media applications until I do everything written on my to-do list for the day (Kushlev, Leitao, 2020).

Playing a few levels on a game that you have on your phone while waiting for something or while relaxing is not a waste of time. But, playing a game right after you use the phone to send an important message or an email is a waste of time. You are losing an hour or half an hour playing your game without realizing it. Trust me, I have been there and I know that you are doing the same thing right now. This is wrong and you should stop immediately if you want to manage your time well. The easiest solution is to delete the games that you have on your smartphone. But you won't learn about control in that way. Leave the games on your smartphone but do not play them while working or performing other important activities.

How Can You Use Your Smartphone to Help You with Time Management?

Now, let's talk about the positive use of smartphones. Smartphones can make people more productive and help them with time management. Remember that time management is not about getting a task done as fast as possible to the detriment of the quality of the work that you produce. It is about completing a task efficiently and effectively in accordance with the standards and objectives set for it (Kushlev, Leitao, 2020).

Your time can be easily managed with alarms and reminders. Alarms and reminders make everything easier because they remind people about important tasks. They also have the power to prevent people from thinking about other tasks because they force them to keep working on the current ones. Often, they serve as task-switching cues so that people can avoid the detrimental effects that multi-tasking will have on their management of time.

Schedules were mentioned in the chapters above, but I will dedicate a small paragraph about them here as well, simply because there are many applications available online that allow you to create daily schedules. It is actually quite simple. You need to open the calendar on your smartphone and implement tasks and appointments for each day. If you decide to do this, do not forget to schedule important breaks.

People can use their smartphones to create "to-do lists." They can also plan and write notes on the go. By creating an ongoing to-do list or a planning note on their smartphone, they have the ability to add to it whenever things pop into their heads.

Smartphones have the power to synchronize peoples' calendars, contacts, and to-do lists across numerous devices. For instance, people are going to be able to sync their smartphones with their iPads and home and work computers. This means that whatever people add to their smartphones will automatically appear on their other devices. Once you do this, you need to train yourself to implement every meeting, invitation, event, and deadline on your smartphone as soon as you are alerted to it.

Smartphones allow people to call other people all the time but this does not mean that you need to be permanently accessible. You should not answer your phone while working unless you're waiting for an important work call. Taking calls all the time is multitasking and it interrupts people. Additionally, it affects peoples' productivity. Turn your phone's sound off to ensure that you are not disturbed. This way, the caller is given the opportunity to leave a voicemail that you can deal with later. Alternatively, if you need to take some calls but not others, your smartphone can be programmed to ring if certain contacts are trying to call you but remain silent for all others.

It is important to mention that it would be foolhardy to expect to achieve smartphone use minimalism overnight. However, a combination of the above tips has helped me greatly and I am sure that it would do the same thing for you.

Chapter 11

Effective Time Management Principles, Techniques, and Tips

YOU CAN'T MAKE UP for lost time. You can only do better in the future. After all, you are here to improve your time management skills. Luckily for you, I know the best ways that could assist you. As I mentioned in the introduction, I know they are the real thing that could help you because I have practiced and implemented them myself.

Time management is not a talent that you are born with. Yes, you need an amazing set of DNA to do math like an expert or sing opera music, but with time management, you can work your way up to the highest level without having an "efficiency" gene. Successful time management is a matter of habit and it requires sacrifices and some specific principles, techniques, and tips. In this chapter, I present to you the best ones (Dunford, Tamang, 2014).

The Pareto Principle

The Pareto principle or the 80/20 principle tells us that in any population, some things are likely to be much more important than others. A good benchmark or hypothesis is that 80% of results or outputs flow from 20% of causes and sometimes from a much smaller proportion of powerful forces.

This principle should be used by everyone in their daily life. It should also be used by every organization and group. It can help individuals and groups achieve much more with much less effort. The 80/20 principle can raise personal effectiveness and happiness. It can increase the profitability of corporations and the effectiveness of organizations. It even holds the key to raising the quality and number of public services while cutting their cost. This book is written from a burning conviction, validated by personal and business experience, that this principle is one of the best ways of dealing with and transcending the pressures of modern life.

In 1906, Italian economist Vilfredo Pareto created a mathematical formula to describe the unequal distribution of wealth in his country (Dunford, Tamang, 2014). Pareto observed that 20% of the people owned 80% of the nation's wealth. He could not know it, but in time that rule would be found to apply with uncanny accuracy to many situations and be useful in many disciplines, including the study of business productivity.

In the late 1940s, Dr. Joseph M. Juran—a product quality guru of that era—attributed the 80/20 Rule to Pareto and called it the Pareto Principle or Pareto Law. The principle may not have become a household term, but the 80/20 rule is certainly cited to this day to describe economic inequity. It also is a useful tool to help you prioritize and manage your work and life (Dunford, Tamang, 2014).

How can you apply the Pareto principle to gain more time?

The Pareto principle, like the truth, can make you free. You can work less. At the same time, you can earn more and enjoy more free time. The only price is that you need to do some serious 80/20 thinking. This will yield a few key insights that, if you act on them, could change your life (Dunford, Tamang, 2014).

And this can happen without the baggage of religion, ideology, or any other externally imposed view. The beauty of 80/20 thinking is that it is pragmatic and internally generated. It is also centered on the individual.

There is a slight catch. You must do the thinking. You must "edition" and elaborate what is written here for your own purposes. But this shouldn't be too difficult.

The insights gained from 80/20 thinking are not many, but they are very powerful. Not all of them will apply to every reader, so if you find your experience different, skip to the next insight that does resonate with your own situation.

First, if you look closely at the items on your to-do list, chances are only a few are tied to important issues. While it may be satisfying to cross off a large number of the smaller issues, the 80/20 rule suggests that you focus on the more important items that will generate the most significant results. The list might not become much shorter but you will be practicing effective prioritization.

Next, in assessing risks for an upcoming project, you'll find that not every risk carries equal significance. Select the risks that pose the highest potential for damage and focus your monitoring and risk planning activities on them. Don't ignore the others, just distribute your efforts proportionately.

It is also important to note that the objective of 80/20 thinking is to generate actions that will make sharp improvements in your life and that of others. This type of action requires unusual insight. Insight requires reflection and introspection. Insight sometimes requires data gathering. Do this as it relates to your own life. Often, insight can be generated purely by reflection, without the explicit need for information. The brain has much more information than we imagine already.

The Pomodoro Technique

It may seem silly at first, but millions of people swear by the life-changing power of the Pomodoro technique. This may seem silly because pomodoro means tomato in Italian. This popular time management method asks you to alternate pomodoros—focused work sessions—with frequent short breaks to promote sustained concentration and stave off mental fatigue (Cirillo, 2006).

The Pomodoro technique was developed in the late 1980s by then university student Francesco Cirillo (Cirillo, 2006). Cirillo was struggling to focus on his studies and complete assignments. Feeling overwhelmed, he asked himself to commit to just ten minutes of focused study time. Encouraged by the challenge, he found a tomato shaped kitchen timer, and the pomodoro technique was born.

Although Cirillo went on to write a 130-page book about the method, its biggest strength is its simplicity:

1. Get a to-do list and a timer.

2. Set your timer for 25 minutes and focus on a single task until the timer rings.

3. When your session ends, mark off one pomodoro and record what you completed.

4. Then enjoy a five-minute break.

5. After four pomodoros, take a longer, more restorative 15-30-minute break.

The 25-minute work sprints are at the core of the method, but a pomodoro practice also includes three rules for getting the most out of each interval:

1. **Break down complex projects.** If a task requires more than four pomodoros, it needs to be divided into smaller, actionable steps. Sticking to this rule will help ensure you make clear progress on your projects.

2. **Small tasks go together.** Any tasks that will take less than one pomodoro should be combined with other simple tasks. For example, "write the rent check," "set vet appointment," and "read Pomodoro article" could go together in one session.

3. **Once a pomodoro is set, it must ring.** The pomodoro is an indivisible unit of time and cannot be broken, especially not to check incoming emails, team chats, or text messages. Any ideas, tasks, or requests that come up should be taken note of to come back to later. A digital task manager (there are tons of apps on

the Google app store and the Apple store) would ease your job, but pen and paper work fine too.

In the event of an unavoidable disruption, take your five-minute break and start again. Cirillo recommends that you track interruptions (internal or external) as they occur and reflect on how to avoid them in your next session (Cirillo, 2006).

The rule applies even if you do finish your given task before the timer goes off. Use the rest of your time to learn or improve skills or the scope of your knowledge. For example, you could spend the extra time reading professional journals or researching networking opportunities.

The pomodoro technique can be a valuable weapon against the planning fallacy as well. When you start working in short, timed sessions, time is no longer an abstract concept but a concrete event. It becomes a pomodoro—a unit of both time and effort. Distinct from the idea of 25 minutes of general "work," the pomodoro is an event that measures focus on a single task (or several simple tasks).

The concept of time changes from a negative—something that has been lost—to a positive representation of events that were accomplished. I call it "inverting time" because it changes the perception of time from an abstract source of anxiety to an exact measure of productivity. This leads to much more realistic time estimates.

When you use the Pomodoro technique, you have a clear measurement of your finite time and your efforts, allowing you to reflect and plan your days more accurately and efficiently. With practice, you'll be able to accurately assess how many pomodoros a task will take and build more consistent time management habits.

Time Management and Productivity

With time management, every person in this world can increase their focus. As we all know, increased focus improves our productivity like nothing else. It also gives us a chance to capture bigger opportunities. Higher levels of productivity help you get more done in less time and significantly decrease the stress people feel when they have a lot to do.

When you manage your time, you can plan your day and increase your performance. Daily planning improves productivity as well. Planning your time is an important element of time management that increases productivity and effectiveness.

Learn How to Delegate

Track relay is one of my favorite sports to watch, especially during the Olympics. That is because the runners participating make blindly reaching for a baton at 20 mph while staying in their lanes look so easy. However, easy is not a word that describes the situation well. What they are doing is really difficult. The reason why I am impressed by this sport is quite easy to explain. These athletes know how to delegate effectively.

At first, delegating sounds easy, as we have already seen. When I first started organizing my time, I thought it was going to be a piece of cake. I was wrong. "Passing the baton" requires a lot of communication, coordination, and trust.

Delegation is important in time management because you should not do everything yourself. If you learn how to delegate, you will empower the people you work with or live with, you will build trust with them, and you will assist their development as well as yours. For example, if you know how to delegate at work you will do a task in a smaller amount of time. Also, you will divide your chores and you will lower the amount of time you spend on things like cleaning (Cross, 1980).

In order to delegate efficiently, you need to start with the right person for the job, task, or chore. For instance, you need to learn about every strength, weakness, and preference of the person you want to ask for help or assign to a task. Then, you have to explain to them why you want to have them take the task on. It really helps when you explain to people why you are giving them responsibilities. Last but not least, always say thank you. Regardless of whether the task is successful or not, show appreciation and make sure it is genuine and comes from the heart.

Effective Time Management Tips

The upcoming time management tips are crucial steps to stay on track. They are small investments that will pay out in the end and make you able to handle a full day of activities without losing productivity or a significant amount of time (Cross, 1980).

1)Take Care of Your Health and Decrease Stress

Taking care of yourself and your health will help your body rejuvenate, both mentally and physically. When their minds are healthy, people can achieve a lot. Practice managing your time according to your biological clock by scheduling priority tasks during the peak time of the day when your energy levels are at their best.

I suggest engaging in exercise. Do yoga, go jogging, or ride a bicycle. Every time you have done a workout, you will be feeling much healthier and full of new energy—ready to tackle all your tasks for the day.

2)Start Your Day Early

A lot of people are more productive in the morning. That is logical because, after sleep, people have more energy. They are more alert and ready to take on everything they have planned the day before. I do this all the time. For example, if I have one more project or one more task for the day than I normally do, I set my alarm clock a couple of hours earlier than I usually do. Mornings are way more productive for me than staying up late in the evenings. According to my experience so far, mornings can offer people a significant amount of extra time.

3)Always Plan

Every evening, take your smartphone or your notebook and start planning the next day. If this does not sound good for you or if it sounds exhausting, then try doing it every Sunday. Plan your days ahead, invest half an hour in this task and I guarantee you higher productivity and efficiency. While you plan, do not forget to:

- Review all of your commitments.
- Add every personal appointment.
- Add everything that you failed to do on the previous day.
- Identify your top priorities.

4)Never Forget About Your Personal Time Management System

Create or adopt a time management system that works for you. While crafting this time management system, make sure to take into consideration your priorities, tasks, personal meetings, work meetings, and goals. And most importantly, stick to it. Remember, if something does not work, remove it and add something else. This is another simple skill that will make you more efficient and bring a greater return in time.

5)Find a Quiet Place

Noise is not good for us. It distracts us and makes us unable to recharge and relax. When you want to concentrate, look for a quiet place or a quiet time of day. For example, I often go to the nearest park in the mornings to write. It helps me concentrate and accomplish quality work.

6) Say "NO"

Unless it is something really important to you, say "no" as much as you can. I started with saying "no" to tasks that made me feel highly pressured. I decided to save my energy and concentration for tasks that are important to me and I enjoy doing. You should do the same thing. Saying "yes" to a lot of additional tasks can make you feel overwhelmed and interfere with your time management system.

The above principles, techniques, and tips help you excel in meeting your goal and managing your time efficiently. They also improve the time management system process. In the end, remember one thing. Find the difference between interest and commitment. This way, you will become able to keep yourself healthy, stress-free, and organized (Cross, 1980).

Final Words

At the end of this journey, it is safe to say that time management is crucial to today's modern world. Without it, you will only function as a normal adult in a limited capacity. You will always be late with tasks and meetings, you won't be productive, and you will definitely experience chaos every day.

All that can be changed and this book aims to provide you with the help you need. At one point, we all get caught up in the moment and lose our ground, but once you have a plan to push you in the right direction, you will turn out allright.

The information that I included in this book, every principle, technique, and tip can change not only your view of time but also your bottom line and your life. Start every day with small steps. First, focus on what energizes you and makes you improve, even if the improvement is small. For some people, this will be the creation of a to-do list, while for others this will be using the Pareto principle. When you start with small steps, you will increase the chances of managing time effectively and you will feel in control. Of course, you will have more time for yourself and for those closest to you.

Furthermore, the strategy discussed in this book will help you stop procrastinating. However, do not over-schedule yourself. Adding tons of tasks to your day will lead to constant changes, delayed tasks, and feeling overwhelmed. As I mentioned before, take small steps when committing to time management.

Measure your success all the time and create a reward system. Learn from mistakes and do not repeat them. Adjust all the time according to your needs and your time management system's needs. Know your challenges and do everything in your power to prevent them.

This book is the first step towards change and a step closer to effective time management. Yes, changes sometimes can feel uncomfortable but we must focus on the bigger picture. Trust me, this step-by-step plan will help you become more energetic, profitable, confident, relaxed, and efficient. Do not forget to set an example for others. Tell other people about your plans and about your strategies. After all, every single person on this earth can benefit from this book by learning how to manage time.

Remember, in a world where uncertainty reigns, contemplating the future with a time management system has a calming effect. Take advantage of that today and make your life easier.

If you enjoyed this book and the powerful strategies inside, an honest review is always appreciated and will help me reach other readers who struggle with Self Discipline and Time Management like you!

Good Luck on your journey,
your best fan, Steve

Refereces

Duckworth, A. L. (2009). Self-discipline is empowering. Phi Delta Kappan, 90(7), 536.

Duhigg, C. (2020). The Power of Habit. PTS Publishing House.

Ford, L. R. (2007). 101 Ways to Improve Your Health. Lyall Ford.

Gul, F., & Pesendorfer, W. (2001). Temptation and self-control. Econometrica, 69(6), 1403-1435.

Jones, G., Hanton, S., & Connaughton, D. (2007). A framework of mental toughness in the world's best performers. The Sport Psychologist, 21(2), 243-264.

Pashler, H. (2016). Attention. Psychology Press.

Peters, P. S. (2020). Chimp paradox. Ebury Publishing.

Rachman, Stanley J. Fear and courage. WH Freeman/Times Books/Henry Holt & Co, 1990.

The Massachusetts Institute of Technology (MIT). Massachusetts Institute of Technology. (2021, December 26). Retrieved December 26, 2021, from https://www.mit.edu/

Aquila, F. D. (1992). Is There Ever Enough Time?: Twelve Time-Management Tips for Teachers. The Clearing House, 65(4), 201-203.

Cirillo, F. (2006). The pomodoro technique (the pomodoro). Agile Processes in Software Engineering and, 54(2), 35.

Cross, R. (1980). How to Beat the Clock: Tips on Time Management. National Elementary Principal, 59(3), 27-30.

Dunford, R., Su, Q., & Tamang, E. (2014). The pareto principle.

Eccles, J. S., & Wigfield, A. (2002). Motivational beliefs, values, and goals. Annual review of psychology,

53(1), 109-132.

Howland, J. M. (2007). Mental skills training for coaches to help athletes focus their attention, manage arousal, and improve performance in sport. Journal of Education, 187(1), 49-66.

Klingsieck, K. B. (2013). Procrastination. European Psychologist.

Kushlev, K., & Leitao, M. R. (2020). The effects of smartphones on well-being: Theoretical integration and research agenda. Current opinion in psychology, 36, 77-82.

O'Donoghue, T., & Rabin, M. (2001). Choice and procrastination. The Quarterly Journal of Economics, 116(1), 121-160.

www.ingramcontent.com/pod-product-compliance
Lightning Source LLC
Chambersburg PA
CBHW071246070526
44583CB00017B/2345